A Letter to Samuel

CHANDI CHIRWA

An environmentally friendly book printed and bound in
England by www.printondemand-worldwide.com

Mixed Sources
Product group from well-managed
forests, and other controlled sources
www.fsc.org Cert no. TT-COC-002641
© 1996 Forest Stewardship Council

PEFC Certified
This product is
from sustainably
managed forests
and controlled
sources
www.pefc.org
PEFC/16-33-415

This book is made entirely of chain-of-custody materials

http://www.fast-print.net/bookshop

A LETTER TO SAMUEL
Copyright © Chandi Chirwa 2015

A catalogue record for this book is available from the
British Library

ISBN 978-178456-217-5

First published 2015 by FASTPRINT PUBLISHING
Peterborough, England.

Foreword

Dear Samuel,

There is so much I want to share with you, so many things I want you to see and understand. I know I don't have enough words to say, I don't even know where to start. They say life is what you make it....son, what life brings can sometimes make you. Therefore I present to you this letter, as my life has been so much influenced by circumstances. It's been said, its better caught than taught, but I feel inadequate to teach you, I would love to say do as I do but, in the paradox of life, I find myself doing stupid things and making decisions that have no reasoning.

That's why I write this letter, it's not a 'how to' letter. But more than anything I want you to understand that there is more to life than what you see with your physical eyes. I finally agree that nothing in life is black and white. I hope this letter will encourage you to see beyond the four walls, to stir up the gift that is within you. I hope God will show you the things He has shown me for His glory.

I don't know if I am blessed or cursed because of the things I have seen and experienced, but one thing I do know, is that they draw me closer to God. They might be one hundred reasons to explain, the things I have been through or seen, but there is no science text book, not a logical explanation or definition of what I have experienced.

In Wikipedia it says this: Early researchers tried to establish a link between déjà vu and serious mental disorders such as schizophrenia, anxiety, and dissociative identity disorder, but failed to find the experience of some diagnostic value. There does not seem to be a special association between déjà vu and schizophrenia or other psychiatric conditions.

The reason they came to this wrong conclusion is simply their understanding of déjà vu.

The general understanding of déjà vu is this: Déjà vu, from French, literally "already seen", is the phenomenon of having the strong sensation that an event or experience currently being experienced has been experienced in the past, whether it has actually happened or not.

So how would you feel if five years of your life flashes in front of your eyes in a space of five minutes or your dreams come to life in the same week? Samuel, I have been in situations where déjà vu was so clear, I was not sure whether I was dreaming or living, it's also known as precognition, according to Wikipedia in parapsychology, precognition (from the Latin, "before" "acquiring knowledge"), also called future sight, and second sight, is a type of extrasensory perception that would involve the acquisition or effect of future information that cannot be deduced from presently available and normally acquired sense-based information or laws of physics and nature.

A Letter to Samuel

Young Days

I was born in Mzimba, the district of Mzuzu; I must have had the best time of my life in Katoto, that's where we moved as a family. My mother left me with granddad and grandma at the age of 2, to study in the UK. Funnily enough my cousins were also left by their parents....my cousins are my brothers and sisters to me, Chikondi, Mime, Paul, Lojenzo, Aunt Thandi, and Uncle Sydney, we all lived under one roof. All of our parents were living in some part of the world. My dad lived the other side of town. By the way I never called him dad, I called him uncle. He lived in his own place near town, 15 miles from granddad and grandma's house. And when he used to come round, every one shouted "asbwen, asbwen" which means uncle, feeling the odd one out I joined them.

Time to time I would go round his house in Zolo Zolo, it was here in Zolo Zolo, that the precognition was clear as day light, I must have been round the age of 4.

I remember waking up in the morning in my dad's bed, where I was sleeping was right next to the window, it was a clear blue Malawian sky. I moved the net curtain slightly, because I could hear children playing, as I looked through the window I saw a small boy and a little girl, at the top of the drive way, laughing and joking, and the little boy pushed the girl into the bush, at that moment the boy froze, and looked directly at me, as thou he saw me move the net curtain, as he looked at me instantly, I realized it was me.

There I was watching myself playing with Mimi. I watched through the window to see what I was going to do, and all of a sudden Mimi got up and pushed me over. They continued playing and I continued watching. The little boy would stop and stare in my direction, at one moment I saw the girl looking at my direction she asked, "What are you looking at?" My dad then walked in the room. I quickly forgot about the incident. It must have been weeks later I was with Mimi in my dad's house we pinched some sweets from the kitchen and we ran to the top of the driveway to eat our sweets. We then started playing, Mimi was near a big bush I pushed her and she went flying into the bush, I started laughing, at that moment I felt like someone was watching me, I looked at my dad's window, to see if he was watching me, but he wasn't. As we played I couldn't shake this feeling that someone was watching. I tried looking through the window to see, but then Mimi pushed me. As I was on the floor, I had the déjàvu sensation, I quickly got up, looked at the window, and it occurred to me that I was looking through the window and I was watching myself.

Moments like this I will never forget. And that was neither the first nor the last. Mimi and I were best friends, you could not separate us. We walked to school holding hands, play mum and dad games.

Now our relationship is different, before I moved to the UK, she moved from our home in Mzuzu to live with her mum in Lilongwe. First time I went back to Mzuzu to visit grandma, Mimi visited for few hours, she was in town, all we said to each other was hi. She had become such a beautiful girl, but it felt like there was something separating us, I don't know if it was the language barrier as I was more familiar with English now, rather than the mother tongue, or if it was the fact that she was abused by one of our uncles and I was there, and I couldn't protect her, and the guilt of not being able to stop him from harming her. I wondered if she thought about me, why I was not talking, but at the same time I wondered about her why is she not talking to me. We were like strangers.

Growing up in Malawi, to me was simply fun.

Everyone knew the Chirwa family. Though we lived amongst the poorest people in the world, we were not too bad. Yes, we had no taps for fresh running water, no electricity or flushing toilets. We were happy. We would walk miles to fetch clean running water.

I remember one night Chikondi and Paul went to get water for bathing and breakfast in the morning. My friend and I followed, when we arrived at the house, being pitch black, the owner of the house turned on the lights, my friend was in a shock, he had never seen anything like this before. He said to me "Chandi, how can God be real, if man can generate moon how can God be real" his face was so amazed, as he gazed at the light bulb. He really thought it was the moon. I feel like the apostle Paul when he said in Phil. 4:12 "I know how to be abased and I know how to abound." Everywhere and in all things I have learned both to be full and to be hungry, both to abound and to suffer need. We were not poor. It just happened that we were living with the poorest people in the world.

So here I will take time to remind you to thank God for everything you have. Living in the UK makes you one of the richest people in the world, believe me. I remember in Malawi we had no flushing toilets, our toilet was a hole outside the house; as you do your business you would see lizards, spiders, all sorts of creepy crawlies. I used to light a piece of paper and throw it down the hole, and you could see all the maggots and poo, lol, it was nice! As I mentioned before water was not an easy thing to come by, Uncle Sydney used to work for the fire department, once in a while he would bring the fire truck to the house and, boy, we would fill our buckets with water, people from the village would gather round our house with buckets.

In the end we got our own tap outside the house and we sold water. 30t per bucket, all depending on how big the bucket was. So please be happy with what you have, you have no idea how blessed you are.

Take advantage of education, and the easiness of having access to the learning material. My school was outside on a sandy ground, with a small board nailed to the wall. Katoto public school was a joke.

It was my first school and I enjoyed every moment there. Not because I was learning but the fun we used to have. I remember when civil war kicked off (called Operation Bwzani), my friend Wisdom and I, were counting cars. You see from my class you could see the main road, the game was simple you choose left or right, whichever side has the most cars coming out, wins. I usually chose the left, it was coming out of the town, and the right side was going into town. In those days Mzuzu did not have many cars. We would normally count about 20 cars in one lesson. On the day of the civil war we were counting the cars, but all along we could hear noises of fire and explosions, no one knew what it was, while the noises got louder and louder and closer.

My side of the road seemed fruitful, I was winning, and then it got really strange because there were so many cars leaving town I lost count: it was a line of cars; we had never seen anything like it. Wisdom and I stood up in shock with our mouths wide open. At that moment we noticed it was not just cars, there were people running, the whole class stood up, now the noise was louder and closer. The teacher shouted out, "Children please sit down". Another student pointed out to the teacher, "Look those men are setting those houses on fire". "Please sit down", not knowing what to do, the teacher tried to keep us calm, until people began running across to the school. One child shouted to someone he recognized, that man ran back, picked up the child and ran for his life. The teacher tried shouting once more, "Kids sit down". Another kid shouted out, "Look, soldiers". At the word soldiers, the sound of machine guns began blazing, in a flash there was so much anarchy and noise I have never experienced again.

As I watched the panic and fear there it was, the déjà vu sensational, I gazed at the children running in panic, I gazed at the teacher screaming for her life, and all I could think about was is it a dream, the same dream again? "I guess I am going to wake up now". Sadly I didn't, Wisdom was now shouting at me, "Why are you just standing there, let's run Chandi, run". There was no hint of fear in me, the guns got louder, now we could see soldiers throwing grenades at the house near the school. The sound of guns filled the air. "Run Chandi", I had no fear, I have seen this before and it's going to be okay, but I could not tell him, I couldn't bring myself to talk. Then I just said "Pick up the pens", he then started picking up all the pens and said "Well done Chandi now I know why you didn't run". He was happy because pens did not come easily. We used to write on the floor because we had no pens. If you had a pen you could write on a piece of paper. Now the plan was to go to our friend's house to show off our pens. I felt sorry for the children who lived in town, because that's where the action was. We lived in the village, no action there.

On the way home the déjà vu was strong. I then began to have more precognition; I was thinking in English and talking English, even though at that age, I could not even speak a word of English. With all that was taking place, on that road home people running, guns firing, the smell of fear and death in the air. All I could see was me speaking to my friends in England, telling them the story of the war in Malawi. The idea of being in England excited me.

This was not the first time that I had precognition of me being in England. The clearest time and most probably the most precognition that has had an impact on me was in Katawa, 5 miles from Zolo Zolo, my dad moved there for some reason. Now I was bit older, I had more freedom to go to my dad when I wanted and live where I wanted. I lived in Katawa with dad, because it was easier for me to get to my new school Vipya private school. I was there before I moved to England. Most of my new school friends, funny enough, lived in Katawa. One night a group of them came to my dad's house to pick me up. We went to see a Jesus film that was being shown, at the football field, by a local church.

I had never seen a screen that big, nor had I ever seen a film before. All the children sat at the front, I was very querulous to know what was happening; to be honest I did not understand why I was there and what I was doing. So I kept asking my friends what is this? They kept saying "A film,it's going to be a film."

And so the film started. During the whole film, all I was watching was my life in England, right on the big screen, and boy it looked scary, I could not believe how old and how big I was. This was not déjà vu, this was not emotions, it was not a feeling, it was my eyes watching my life on a big screen.

I was there working in the Westcliff casino, I was there with your mum; I looked to see if the others were seeing what I was seeing. I asked my friend again, "What is this?" "It's a film about God, have you not seen it?"

It was strange watching myself speaking English and in the casino uniform. The main thing that concerned me about what I was seeing is how big I was. After that, I did not like the idea of growing up.

That moment has affected me up today. (What the heck happened there?) But again it was not the first nor is it the last. I had a dream, I was with my friend at the pond, we were washing our faces, and he was telling me that he fell in the pond, as he was explaining to me that he fell in the pond, he went to show me how, and in showing me how, he actually fell in again. In my dream I could see and hear very clearly what was happening. When he fell in the pond I saw myself standing up, then I saw his sister shouting at me. For some reason in the dream I could not hear what she was saying or know why I was just standing there. In my dream this was from the back view, all the other part was in 3d (yes, I could see from all angles). I can't remember waking up from that dream, but all I remember next, I was with my friend playing near the pond. He said to me "Chandi come over here let me show you where I almost drowned". We went to the pond, we knelt down and he started washing his face and I joined him, he then began telling me the story of how he fell in the pond – as he was telling me the story I was so confused I thought I was still dreaming. He then went to show me how he fell in, and so it happened, he actually fell in. At that moment I stood up, in utter mystification as I watched him drowning. His sister came running over pulled him out, and started shouting at me, "Why are you just standing here watching him drown you evil child, you wanted him to die." I was speechless; I thought I was still dreaming. I walked home that day, in fear, it was as though my life was not real, like I was in a virtual world, and someone was controlling me.

I never told anyone back then the things I was seeing or experiencing, maybe it's because I was too young, maybe it's because I didn't understand, and I didn't understand, so many times these experiences were happening to me, my life was like one big dream.

When I was told that my grandmother was not my mother, rather my grandmother, it never made sense. "Where is mum then?" I would ask.

"Your mum is in England". When mum came to visit, the whole house would be excited. "Chandi's mum is coming". The house would be cleaned over and over and I would ask again and again, trying to make them realise that they were wrong, my grandmother was my mum. In the end they said "Yes you're right Chandi, your auntie is coming", that made sense to me. So dad was uncle, mum was auntie. It was not until I moved to the UK that mum became mum. Even though we had a big picture in grandma's house of my mum and dad; I thought it was all a dream. I have a mum in England? The way Malawians describe England, it's like heaven on earth – the country of honey and milk, there is no poverty or suffering, where everyone is forever happy.

If you were to compare Malawi to the UK, UK is heaven. That's how we viewed England. Many times Malawi has been named the poorest country in the world by the health report. And to me it did not matter, those were my young days. Full of joy, pure happiness, and no worries but also it was very mysterious. If there was anything dark in me in my young days it was fear, fear of death, fear of witchcraft. And of course one thing you can't escape in Malawi, is death.

I have lost many aunties and uncles, in the night it took me a long time to get to sleep, because if you listened to the silence of the night, far in the distance you would hear women wailing, somewhere in the village someone has died every night. Granddad is continually going to funerals, at least once a week.

Because death was always in my face, alone at night that thought was always in my head, "One day I will not be here. When I die I am not going to exist. I just can't imagine that". No one can understand the idea of them not existing and that is simply because God made us to exist for eternity, heaven or hell. Anyway I will save the preaching for later.

It was at Katoto School, I picked up the fear of flying. In the same class, sitting there with Wisdom once again, we decided to skip the lesson after break and went into town. The school is about 15min walk from the town centre. On the way to town Wisdom shouted "Look!" We could both hear a plane, it sounded very loud. He could see it but I couldn't, he started running shouting out that the plane has crashed let's go and see. We arrived at a high point that overlooked the market and there it was, a small army plane. To us it was a huge plane. The plane had crashed at the main entrance of the market, five minutes from the airport. So we ran close to see, but we feared it was going to explode as in the movies. It's not like in England when an accident happens, there was no police, no fire crew, just a crashed plane. Thankfully no one was hurt. This plane looked so big my heart jumped with fear, my hair stood up and I thought of Uncle Ian, he is a pilot. Since that day flying for me has never been easy.

At least once a month a witch doctor would come into the village. Usually he would come and do his dance, drums would be playing, people singing and normally the house would be packed; no room for anyone to move, all watching the doctor doing his dance, he would normally wear bells and shackles round his wrist and ankles. The dance would have no pattern, every five minutes a woman would scream and shake, like she is feeling the spirit. I would attend a lot of these meetings, usually I was there to play with my friends and have a laugh with the girls.

At one time, a meeting took place in the daytime, which was unusual, because they usually took place in the night. After the dancing the witch doctor said to the crowd, "Let's go". My friends and I were playing in the background, but when the crowd started walking with intent, we quickly realized something was up and we realized that this meeting was for the purpose of catching those who practice witchcraft. We arrived at a small mud hut and there the elders walked in with a large group of men. They brought out three pots, and anxiously walked back to the house where it all started. I was then tuned in; I wanted to know what was going on. The village chief began shouting out, "Please sit down and no children." The more he said no

Children the more I wanted to see what was up, so I decided to break away from my friends, and sneaked to a place where I would draw no attention. I sat near the front and I could see everything. Now I know why they said no children, up to this day, what I saw shocks my brain waves, defiles my understanding of everything I know. For weeks I could not sleep. After we all sat down and the chief began explaining, "These three men" (the three men were at the front, looking at the ground. Only fear and terror was on their faces) "What did the three men do", I wondered. He continued, "These three men fly across the world in these three pots". After a long talk, he asked the men to confirm that what he was saying was true, all three men nodded their heads in agreement. Then he asked them to confess and speak out and tell the people how they did it. I can't remember exactly what the three men said but they were asked to show these things that helped them to fly. I don't know what the men did but out of the pots came along strange looking things, my best way of describing of what I saw was like three cat tails, no hair, no mouth, no eyes, but the more you looked you could sense they had eyes, noses and ears . Even today logically I cannot explain what came out of those pots and bearing in mind the pots where empty beforehand.

It must have been months later my friends and I were playing in the dark, outside dad's video show, (Malawi version of cinema, VCR and a small TV), and about 30ft in the sky, a fireball flew by. "Wow," we shouted. We tried chasing it, but there it went, too fast for us and too amazing to ever forget: a fire ball flying in the skies of Katoto. And I knew exactly what it was.

Malawi is much known for its witchcraft and black magic. Bank robbers would come all the way from South Africa, to get magic potions, which would keep them alive in shootouts with police, or potions to make money quickly, basically whatever you needed or wanted Malawi had it. My friend's dad Yotam was one of the people who made those potions for the people's needs. Even I nearly went to him, after five years of living in the UK, my life was about violence, fights and gang battles. I desperately needed a potion that would make my fist as hard as rock so I could punish my enemies. After going back to Malawi for holiday, I asked my friend to arrange it, it was ready for me but at the last minute I chickened out. And I thank God I did, I can't imagine the spiritual side effects after doing things like that.

The picture that I will never forget, when dad was taking this picture, I remember his smile. At that very moment he walked up to me to stand me up straight into a position and as he walked back, from the corner of my eye I saw the Mickey Mouse ears on my glasses, I knew it was Mickey Mouse. We never had television back then, let alone watched Mickey Mouse. I looked down and I saw the badge on my jumper, it reminded me of my future college, in the UK, South-east Essex college. At that moment not only was I seeing myself in this future college, but I was thinking like an adult, I was thinking in English. I don't think I was even able to talk when the picture was taken but in my head, I was doing more than talking.

It was then, I looked at my dad and I said to myself this very man taking the picture is my dad and he's going to die.

I then started crying out loud, he came running and picked me up.

Samuel, when you were young, I watched you cry for no reason, I watched you talk, as though you were speaking to someone only you can see, and every time you would do something strange, in my mind I understood. I write this letter in hope to make it clear to you, if you experience any of the things I mentioned, talk to me.

The last days of my life in Malawi, did not make sense, it all happened too quickly. Being only 10 years old, nothing made sense, it all happened too fast.

I remember walking with dad to have my picture taken; dad said it was for my passport photo, so I could go to

England. At dinner times we usually ate with our hands but all of a sudden it stopped, they wanted me to practice eating with a knife and fork, I started laughing, I thought it was a joke, "Who eats with a knife and a fork?" I laughed so much my granddad rebuked me, saying, "Chandi if you are going to be living in England with white people you must learn to eat with a knife and fork". So I tried it, it was like trying to eat rice with chop sticks, it was impossible, I could not do it, I gave up. After so many attempts, granddads said, "Okay, eat with your hands boy." And I was set free.

Paul and I would stay up late, playing cards until the candle would burn out. It was those times we would talk about England, Paul would say so many things about England; games, toys, playing, clothes, this and that, hanging out with white people, boy it would be so cool, "You're so lucky Chandi".

I didn't care about those things, deep down I was thinking, "Wow, I get to meet my mum". I wondered about my mum, what is she like, is she going to shout at me, how does she sound when she speaks, and what does she look like? I was so excited about meeting mum.

Samuel, my generation is full of broken families, and your generation is going to be worse, because that's how it is, sin abounds. And I pray that you would be a Godly man, a man of character and self control. One who will look after his family? Listen son, more than anything, more than the earth has to offer, children want their mum and dad, more than bling, or any material possession, children want a relationship with their parents. At the care home, we looked after 90 year olds, some 98 and they all still cry for mum and dad. If you are going to be a dad, be a dad.

As much as I love all those who have looked after me, I would be a different man today, if those early years were spent with mum and dad.

Finally I was told by dad, "Tomorrow be ready, you will be going to Lilongwe, and there you will get on a plane". "Wow, a plane": fear, excitement all in one.

The day I was leaving Mzuzu, I had an argument with Paul, even though he was older than I, he was jealous and angry at me. He said I didn't deserve to be going to England. Me leaving was a big thing to my family members, now people were moving on, everyone was leaving the grandma and granddad's home. Lonjezo and Mimi had already gone and Paul was leaving the following week. That day I traveled with dad and Chikondi, who was going to Blantyre polytechnic university. Chikondi was the golden boy, everything he did was great, football, basketball, school, everything he touched turned to gold and, what a surprise, he is now a lecturer at the very same university he went to study.

On that bus, we laughed and joked, deep down I was upset and I knew that from that point, life was not going to be the same. I can still hear the voice of Chikondi as he was jumping off the bus, he shouted out: "Bye Chandi! Write to me."

Dad and I stayed in Lilongwe for a day or two and at the airport; dad gave me his speech…..

1. Look after mum

2. Behave yourself

3. Do what mum tells you, and

4. Be a good boy

During the speech my mind was in a panic mode, "What does mum look like?" He gave me a cuddle, pointed out where I should go and off I went. At the age of ten years old, life was about to become one big dream.

Welcome to England

H oney and milk, and so it was, the plane was massive, I was so excited and the scent of the plane so fresh, so sweet, Katoto never smelled like this. People sleeping, some had head phones, I was like wow. The air hostess was giving out drinks, the person next to me had a can of coke, then she put one on my little table, "Wow, what is this?" I had never seen a can of coke in my life, I knew it was coca cola, but I had never seen it like this before, in Malawi it was always in a glass bottle and in order for you to buy one, and you have to give the shop an empty bottle. I had no idea how to open the thing, I couldn't wait to open it, and so I waited for the person next to me to open theirs, so I could copy them. They took forever. Finally he cracked it open and I thought wow, that looks so cool and it sounds cool. Now it's my turn and I could not do it, I was hoping the people next to me would see that I was struggling, and offer help. In the end I broke the opener. I pointed it out to the lady who gave it to me, she asked me if I wanted another one, I thought she asked me, "Did you pay for it", so I shook my head and she walked off. She never came back with my can of coke. Now I was upset, and scared realizing these people don't understand me, and I don't understand them. All night I thought about the can of coke. I really wanted to taste it.

Nevertheless I was buzzing, eventually despite my excitement I fell asleep. In the morning the sun was shining through the small window and for a second I thought I was in heaven, literally above the clouds, I could not believe it. When we took off, it was night I could not see anything outside, but now I could see these clouds, I wanted to touch them.

It was a smooth landing at Heathrow airport, it was 28thAug 1995. I will never forget walking through the airport, it was spectacular. I was amazed, then a lady took me and some other children and said a few things that I didn't understand, but I gathered she meant she would look after me. She first took us to the luggage section where I recognized my suitcases going round on the belt, I chased them down and around, I saw a few people laughing. The lady tried telling me not to worry, they would come back round. I took no chances.

After we collected our luggage, she gave us another talk. This time I understood the word 'Mum', and we all followed the lady. We came to a corner and all of a sudden, I saw hundreds of people, all waiting to pick someone up. Some of the children who were with us began to disappear; parents or relatives picked them up. The lady turned to me "Can you see your mum?" Not knowing how to answer I just did the foreign thing, nodded my head. I panicked because I thought I had to point my mum out, but I couldn't recall what she looked like, so I started thinking, "They're going to send me back, because I can't find my mother". I thought "Dad is going to kill me; he is going to say, could you not remember her from the picture?" As I was thinking, these three women came running up to me screaming my name in excitement, Auntie Derewe, Auntie Feskaine and of course mum. But which one was mum?

The journey to Southend-on-Sea was long. It was raining and grey being British weather. In the car loud talking and laughing, they wanted to know how good my English was, so they tested me, "Where is your arm?" "Where is your leg?" "Where is your nose?" "Well done", and that's all I knew. I sat in the back watching and trying to figure out which one was mum, it was quite simple, I knew it was her.

Before arriving home, we stopped over at Auntie Janet's house. More people, more talking, more laughing. I fell asleep and off we went. We finally arrived home, Salisbury Avenue. My first home in the UK.

It was a two bedroom flat, shared by the three women. And now it had a ten year old boy. I quickly began to enjoy the luxury of living in UK with flushing toilets, inside bath, wow, I loved baths it was so cool. I didn't have to make my own toys; battery powered cars, oh my days. My first time at the sea front I realized why Paul was jealous. Car games, shooting games and things we never even dreamed of in Malawi, and, of course, a TV in the house. Children's TV and cartoons were so boring. I was used to watching Rambo, Jackie Chan, Chuck Norris and Van Damme; he was my hero. Oh son, don't worship man. It was here I began to have idols in my heart. please don't be stupid and idolize men, actors, singers and rappers, it's all folly, absolutely stupid.

A few days later, I met Uncle Harry, Auntie Dorothy and their daughter Chimwemwe who's actually my niece. Auntie Dorothy took Chimwemwe and I to the cinema; my first time ever and we saw Casper. The film didn't make sense, I thought it was about a cloud, but that didn't matter because I was amazed enough, just by watching something on a large screen.

After a few weeks I was introduced to Uncle Andrew, who's now married to Auntie Feskani. You see in our culture everyone is an auntie or an uncle, whether they're related or not. Then I was introduced to Uncle Dom, who was really mum's special friend, should

I say. He was great. Uncle Dom would take me to the park, we played football, he took me to the sea front, played games, etc., he gave me time and most of all, he bought me a doner kebab which I regarded as meat from heaven.

I don't know how to explain this part to you, because even I am still confused. Mum had a special friend who I called Uncle Dom, dad had a special friend I called auntie so and so. When dad came to visit us, uncle Dom did not come round unless it was a massive gathering of Malawians. Mum would ask me if auntie so and so would sleep in the same room as dad. I remember my friend in school, Raymond Cooper, asked me "Chandi how many rooms is your flat?" At that time it was in Hermitage Road, "2 bed flat" I said. And the conversation went on, he asked me, "How many people live there?" And my reply was "Hmm, me, mum and Uncle Dom" and he went on to ask "Where does Uncle Dom stay then?" I said "Sometimes in the front room, sometimes in mum's room". He still went on by asking, "So where does your mum sleep then?" Then I replied "Hmm, in the same room", and then he said "What, your uncle and mum are in the same room?" That's when I had to explain "No Ray, he is not my real uncle, he is mum's special friend". "Oh I see, why do you call him uncle?" I would just end by saying, "Shut up man".

It was times like this that made me feel disconnected from my family, I felt like I had no family simply because I did not understand how mum and dad lived and, of course, no questions were asked.

I was looking forward to going back to Malawi and telling everyone the things I had seen and done. I kept some sweets for my friends; little did I know that it wasn't going to be until three years later that I would see Malawi again.

I remember the day mum told me I was going to start school in Chalkwell Hall. I had mixed feelings, looking forward to the fun in school but at the same time I felt fear, I couldn't speak English, how was I going to make friends. Then I thought how about my friends and family in Malawi? What about Mimi, Paul, Chikondi, Owen, Lonje, am I not going to see them again? At that moment I wanted to be back in grandma's house with all my cousins. It was the place where I felt secure. Here I felt like a stranger.

The first day in Chalkwell Hall was full of amazement, so many classrooms and they were all indoors.

I remember one time I decided to go down stairs, to a place where I knew I was not allowed to go to. They had a big fish tank with so many fishes with all different colures, I thought it was witchcraft, fish in a tank. In Malawi we went fishing for dinner. Fish in a tank, it didn't make sense, but it was so beautiful, as I gazed at the tank, I had déjà vu. It was when I was in Malawi preparing to come to the UK, I had seen myself looking at the tank. I saw myself gazing at the beauty of the fish. Lost in my own world I then heard a voice, you're not allowed down here.

It was not long before I began making friends even with my little English; people liked this little African boy. Because of my English they gave me a little helper a girl called Nicola, I wish I knew her last name, she looked after me telling those off who wanted to pick on me, she helped me with my work, or rather did it for me. Kaser Shik became a good friend, Bradley Watson and Jack Buston loved the way I beat up people, that's another story. A girl called Charlotte became a good helper also. My niece Chimwemwe went to the same school as me, but I didn't realise until a long time after (me being stupid). My first little fight was with a big boy, Ali Hussain, he is now a drug dealing gangster, from good boy to bad boy. It was my fight scenes that made me more popular among the boys, soon everyone wanted to be my friend. That's how I met a guy called Ben Couch, at one time I beat up four boys, then Ben came over with a big smile saying, "Yes brother you beat up three boys, you're hard, you're hard", I had no idea what he was saying. I nodded my head in agreement. He walked off. Five minutes later he came back pushing me and shouting "You beat up my something, something, and someone." Judging by his attitude and red face, I knew he was not happy. He then pushed me again and I quickly went into action and performed the monkey, jumped in the air scratched his face as many times as I could and before my feet touched the ground he was on the floor crying. And he became my fifth victim; I guess the fourth was his relative.

In Malawi we used to go into the jungle and teach each other kung fu, we used to call it ku dealer.

Those fighting skills I learnt in the jungle, were only for Chalkwell School, when I got into the bigger school, there was no time for roundhouse kick, or flying kicks or monkey styles. The fights I had in Chalkwell School were playground fights; the fights in Prittlewell School changed the course of my life.

I started Chalkwell Hall in year six and it went by very quickly. My thinking was still innocent and African. Every day mum would try to get me to speak English. I got by through just nodding my head. In my heart I was waiting for the day I would return to Malawi. Learning English or anything else for that matter was not on the agenda. I am a very slow learner and education never appealed to me. In this area, I wish that you are much better than me.

Now the teachers were preparing us for a big school. They could not prepare me for a life full of violence, drugs, alcohol abuse and a totally bewildered mindset. And that is exactly what was waiting for me.

Chandi Chirwa

The Prittlewell School
(high school)

With innocence and an African mindset, year seven was fun. Still playing with toy guns walking into McDonalds with a sheriff badge and two pistols, I was so cool. You couldn't stop me. When I was walking round town some people laughed, some kids said it looked cool. The bus driver wanted to charge me for an adult ticket, he thought I was over 16 and then he rolled his eyes back when he saw my pistols and agreed I was a child.

I thought Chalkwell was big. This school was really big. It had different classrooms for every subject, science was downstairs, math's upstairs, I could not believe it. Here I am, from a classroom that was a tree outside, to a school with unimaginable classrooms and sports facilities. It was amazing; not to mention computers, I didn't even know what they were.

My first friend was Daniel Martin, to the eyes of the school; he was a geek, to me a friend. I never understood anything he said and I don't think he understood anything I said. It was in the computer room I met my first best friend Glen Strothard, I was talking to Kaiser (we knew each other from Chalkwell Hall) and Glen started laughing at him, so I joined him. From there our hearts were knitted and a year later we became the naughtiest two in our class, Miss Pitts banned us from sitting together for a whole year. By then Daniel Martin had become a geek to me, I was now able to recognize geeks and cool kids, my eyes were open.

So of course Aaron Strothard (the twin brother of Glen) became my friend. It was not long before the best friend list began to grow. On my way home to Hermitage Road, I would meet two boys Daniel Allen aka Boob and Chris Perce, I would see them pass by near my house or see them walk to school. One day I decided to speak to them and Boob invited me to his house and that was it, four years later we were planning suicide at 12.00. Ten years later Chris and I were Bible bashing, preaching in the streets "Jesus loves you." Before the Bible bashing, Chris's house was the place to meet, if you had beers, ganja or if you didn't, it was the place to go.

From those two I met Daniel Poole aka Spoon, he got added into the list. Two years later Spoon and I started recording porn on video tapes from the cable channels and sold it in school for 100% profit.

One time there was a school fight in the school corridor, lots of noise so I ran over to see. It was Joe Mascall aka Joe Shanks, smashing up a boy who was bigger than him, James Bell. People had to drag him off James; I thought he was going to kill him. During that fight I looked through Shanks eyes, I knew we were going to be good friends. Six years later I am calling Shanks to support me to protect your mum's friend from her Albanian brothers; Joe sure did smash a bottle on their heads.

In about year nine my enemies' enemy Allan Carroll joined our school as he was kicked out from his school for fighting. News came very quickly to me that Allan Carroll is a hard nut and hates people I hate and he is joining Prittlewell School. I was looking forward to meeting him. Six years later Carroll comes running into my house saying he's being chased by police, after we sent him to pick up some weed on his ped. The police stopped him, so he stopped and whilst the police officer was coming out of his car, Allan kicked the door and quickly drove off on the moped and the chase was on. End of year 10, my mum introduced me to her friend's son Eked, who was fresh from Zimbabwe. Her friend wanted me to show him around and look after him I guess. Five years later she came running and shouting to Chris's house, smashing up one of our boys' car and shouting out, "What have you done to my son?!" She then sent him back to Zimbabwe. We lost our connection for free alcohol, lots of champagne and no more cash for the strip club (because he worked in Co-op, he was the hook up).

Respect to all my teachers, they kept telling me, I will regret not taking school seriously. They were right, I do regret. I laughed and mocked at most of them.

Once Mr. Gosden (one of the teachers in charge of things) took me to a corner, and while he was talking he was digging his finger on my chest I will never forget what he said "Chandi you are the leader of the gang and I am telling you now, if any of your boys smash things up I am coming straight to you." When I told the boys what Mr Gosden said, we all laughed but then Richard Baker said "Actually he's right, you do think you are the leader. I was not a leader, I was just the loudest. Respect to Mr. Symons, the best English teacher ever, when he taught a lesson on 'Of Mice and Men', it was like he was preaching. It must been the only thing I learned in school.

Through Chris and Boob, came my beloved friend Russell Mayo. About twelve years later, I attended his funeral; he died a few weeks after coming out of prison.

The Boys Who Knew Too Little

It was 11:30am; someone was knocking on my door, "What do they want? I'm not going to open it". All my friends knew the rule, you don't come to my house before 12, I am sleeping. This knocking continued so I opened my window from which you could see right outside the main door. It was Russell, "What time you call this Bro? It's not even 12 yet". He looked at me and showed me his middle finger. "Wait I'm coming".

I slid my bedroom door open, quickly checked if mum was home; no she was at work, so I let Russell up straight into my room. Before he even sat down,

Russell asked me "Where is the video tape?" Inside the tape box was all the stuff we used to roll up. He is asking me and showing me a bag of draw, "Look what I got today, man it's nice rock, quite big, my boy done me a deal". My heart leapt with joy, because I had no smoke.

The way Russell rolled those joints was nice. Every morning, I would wake up, and debate with myself, food or a spliff. Today Russell made my decision nice and sweet. By the time I finished getting changed the joint was rolled. We leaned on the window with no problem, mum was not home.

I took the joint from Russell and inhaled it "Yea that's nice" I said, as I was choking. Russell responded with a big grin on his face.

"What's Chris doing man?" he asked me. "I don't know, when we finish this we will go and find out".

The joint was finished and down we went on our way to Chris' house. We pressed the bell, he too looked out of the window and saw our middle fingers. He opened the door and we walked up the stairs, before reaching the top of the stairs, you could smell the weed. Now I was happier, I was more for the weed than the draw, to Russell draw was cheaper and more long lasting. We entered Chris's room, behold a scene of young men talking about nothing that matters, the room was covered in smoke and filled with talk of smoke.

The usual suspects were in the house. Joe, Tinashe, Spoon, Boob, Kieran, Josh, Allan Carroll, Richard Baker,

Bernard and Adrian. The room was covered with so much smoke, that even if you didn't smoke weed, you would have got high.

It was not always like this. Russell and I also used to go bike riding, from Westcliff to Hadleigh Castle and explored the fields on our bikes. Sometimes the boys and I would go to the cinema or swimming. I would also wait for Sunday for the youth club, even though the youth club I attended with Glen and Azz was full of fights, it was all playground stuff. When Boob lived at Hamlet Court Road we used to climb on the roofs and jump on top of people's houses or go to what we used to call mud land, when the river Thames dries out, we used to go right in the middle and threw each other in the mud.

And now here we are red eyes, totally smoked out, waiting for the evening to get drunk and then go out, and hope we don't end up in a fight.

During the smoke time, we would talk about the good old fights we've had. Chris would always remind me of the fight I had with James Wash, and Allan Carroll would talk about fighting Oley Jones. We would remember when James Bins and Chris Matthews helped me against Wash and his friends and then another time they were in a park with a group of people waiting to burn me alive.

We would talk about the Brown brothers, John and Danny Brown, very notorious in Southend and I had bad run ins with John and his friends. Every time we went out, it was nice but rare to come back without fighting someone. On this occasion the main topic was the last fight. We gathered together just as we usually did, this time it was Joe, Chris, Ad, new face in the gang David Hammond, Spoon and me. After our usual smoke and drink at Chris', Ceylon Road, we headed to Lucy Road, going to talk night club. But we never made it there. As we were on the High Street, about to cross the road, next to Royals shopping centre, a group of lads from nowhere surrounded us, and landed a punch on Joe. We all froze with shock and then their big boy, and he was Big, started asking us, one by one "Do you want to fight? Do you want to fight?" I was in shock, it was happening too quickly and I am high and drunk and who are these guys anyway? Joe was bleeding from his nose, everyone said no to the fighting offer. The big boy with all his friends then asked Joe if he wanted to fight, Joe did not answer but looked at me with hesitation wondering if I wanted to fight. I looked at Joe, "When did this happen?" meaning his nose, it was bleeding. "Just now" Joe responded with confusion, after a few seconds it registered in our heads that we were being jumped. In a matter of seconds it kicked off. Joe threw a punch which landed on the forehead of the big boy. I then quickly took over by landing a bottle on his skull; it sent him crashing on the ground, like David's stone that fell Goliath. As he went to the floor I grabbed him, so he fell facing towards the sky and I began showering him with blows to the head. Meanwhile Joe landed a perfect punch on some other man, the punch sent the guy to the floor, bleeding from the nose and eyes, he then passed out. My blows were landing nicely on the big boy, the bottle confused him and I then began shouting, "Die, die, die," all rage came out, I wanted nothing but death. I was so full of anger and hate. A girl passing by came running over shouting, what are you doing to him, at that point he was nothing but a punch bag, I realised how this looked to the girl so I left him. I went looking for Joe, he was standing next to his victim who passed out, I wanted to get my rage out. Joe's victim was flat on the floor with no life in him, I was so full of rage I wanted to get it out so I threw a few punches on him and it felt like I was hitting a pillow. In fact after that I felt sick and ashamed, even though it was them who started, we finished it. But hitting a body that was unconscious made me sick. I later heard from that boy's friend Richard Daily that he was in a coma in hospital.

We sat there and talked about how people should not mess with us. In Chris' room we felt like brothers, in fact the boys made me feel as if I belonged. I remember Uncle Harry telling me, my friends are not always going to be there. He was right, I look at our lives now, and we are different people, sometimes like strangers.

Lesson 1: Samuel, your friends are not always going to be there. Don't follow people around and end up doing stupid things, be very careful in whom you hang out with, the Bible says in Proverbs 27:17 "As iron sharpens iron so one person sharpens another." The people you hang out with will influence you, in all areas.

All we lived for was the here and now. We knew so little about life, no plans, no goals, no aims, no achievement. If things were happening we were there, if it was not we would be in Chris' room smoking weed and you would find me there. Some of us would hang out more together than others, Russell was more with me and Chris, but after this session it would be just Russell and me. So off we went – it was time to get some beers, just Russell and me, we left the boys in their comfort zone. Russell knew a place you could buy 12 bottles of Scorpion beer for six pounds. And the guy never asked us for ID. We picked up the beer, went to Blackdown flats, sat on the stairs and a new session began. This time just the two of us and this was our second home, every weekend we would be here, the stairs of council flats. If not there, then the toilets down the seafront.

Every time it was just Russell and I something inside me would say tell him, Chandi tell him. For a long time, I ignored it. But this time I didn't: "Russell I need to tell you something" "What?" he would ask.

"When you reach the age of 18 you are going to be in jail for stabbing someone."

"F*ck off man. I would never do that, I don't even carry a knife." Now I got it out of my chest, I reminded him every time we were in the flats or just two of us drinking. He was only 15, reaching 18 seemed like it would never happen.

After we finished the crate of beers we headed off to the seafront, teenage hotspot. In the High Street we met

Glen and Azz. As we headed to the sea front, funnily enough almost at the same spot where we had the last brawl, Azz approached me and said, "You see those boys? I heard them saying you think you're hard". Now I was so high and drunk, I swiftly ran towards one of the boys, in my head I thought I jumped really high and performed a super flying kick, only my leg ended up in his hands and he threw a punch, which sent me flying to the floor, smashing my teeth on the pavement and breaking one of my front teeth in half. For a few seconds I passed out, I woke up not knowing where I was and one of my shoes was missing. All of a sudden, I felt a chill on my teeth, like someone was putting ice on it. I then realized half of my front tooth was missing. From nowhere Spoon appeared asking if I was alright and

Shelley Biggs was on the scene. She was shaking her head in disbelief, "Once again, another fight". Shelley and her friends Vicky Frost and Charlotte Poulten were good friends, being girls they knew the latest gossip and who was doing what. Shelley was a great instrument to me (like the time when the boys gathered in the park waiting to burn me, she warned me of their plan and linked me up with their enemies).

There was so much happening at this point, all I wanted was some trainers. I felt a bit sober, but I couldn't find Russell.

In the morning I woke up with a major hangover, as I laid in my bed thinking "What happened to Russell?"

The phone rang, behold it was Russell. "Bro what happened to you? I was looking for you." "I am in hospital man". "No way", "yea I got run over." We both broke out with laughter.

When Russell saw me getting punched to the floor he came running to my rescue, only to get hit by a car.

Lesson 2: No drinks, and Drugs.

Again I would remind Russell when you are 18 you are going to go to jail for stabbing someone "F*ck off man, why do you always say that?" That was his response.

This time he really questioned me, "Why do you say that, really?" I explained to him sometimes I see things before they happen, but this I did not see but I know.

I told him of the time I went to the cinema with Chris, Richard Baker, Glen, Azz and Spoon. We went to see Matrix 1, when the film ended, as the curtains where closing, in a flash I saw the whole of Matrix 2. When we were walking out of the cinema, I was deep in thought, thinking of what had just occurred. I told the boys, "Guys I have just seen Matrix two. Oh my gosh he is going to be flying like superman." I tried explaining to them as much as I could but their response was "Chandi, you are being weird again." So they laughed at me. After telling the story to Russell, he agreed that I was weird.

Many times I would tell the boys of upcoming events and scenarios, in the end it became a joke, especially when I pointed out to them, that they would do this or that and it happened. When I reminded them, they just laughed and said "No you never". Why should they have taken me seriously? I never took myself seriously. Eventually I gave up. Here and there I would see things and I would keep it to myself, "What else can I do?" I remember when the Twin Towers went down in America, two planes crashed into the Twin Tower buildings. When I saw it in my head, before the actual event it did not mean anything to me, but when it was happening in real life I felt so bad, like I should have done something. But what could I do? I am not even in control of this thing. It just happens, like the skies or a window opens and I see through it, then it closes. But what I saw will happen later. "What can I do?"

Smoking weed and drinking, became a way of escaping from my life and the truth is, that's why people drink and take drugs. To escape, to feel free and every time I was sober life was a drag.

Dad Meets Mum

It was Boxing Day 2001, I could not get hold of Russell, but it didn't matter, I was going out with Joe, Josh, Josh's Brother Gutter and Allan Carroll and afterwards we planned to stay at Joe's.

It was Rewind night at Zinc night club, hip hop, reggae, dance hall and it was run by Matt aka DJ Militant. We started drinking before arrival, it was always cheaper. Two hours into the night I was just about able to keep myself upright on the dance floor. I started dancing with this big mixed race girl and as we were dancing, Allen Carroll came rushing over shouting at me, "Tell this boy I am not racist, how can I be racist my dad is black?!" I looked over at the hip hop boy and he was shouting his mouth off, I could tell he was just looking for an excuse to fight, so Allen

Carroll did not waste any time to give him what he wanted, one punch send him flying on the dance floor. So my dance was ruined.

I grabbed Carroll and we started walking straight out. By the time security arrived we were all out. As we exited the club, Joe was being shouted at by some other hip hop boy. He endured his shouting until he said something about his mum: Joe turned around, landed a nice hook, it sent him straight to the ground. I ran over to make sure he didn't get back up and he couldn't, not from that punch, anyway.

We crossed the car park and started walking up the hill going towards Joe's house in Woodgrange Drive. When we got to the top we turned around and we could see a group running towards us; we thought let's run and not fight but Carroll was fuming he wanted blood. All I was thinking about was the dance. Carroll shouted out, "No boys, they only have one more than us", so we waited for them to catch up. I was so drunk I couldn't see straight, it was a standoff, six of them five of us. Looking into each other's eyes, they hesitated. So they should have, they thought we would be scared, little did they know we do this every week.

Carroll made a war shout, "Come on then!" He ran straight into the pack, grabbed two of them but one pulled out a bottle smacked Carroll on the head. That didn't move him, then I ran up hoping I wouldn't get bottled, started shouting and throwing punches, I didn't even know if they were landing. All I knew, my head was spinning and I then thought I was

Bruce Lee and started making Bruce Lee noises. My boys battered the guys, one of them begged Carroll to stop hitting him, when he did he pulled up his hip hop jeans and ran off and then they all ran for their lives. We immediately started laughing; we never had a fight so easy.

Carroll was not happy that we took so long to attack and that's why he thinks the bottle landed on him.

We went back to Joe's house and Carroll was not satisfied, neither was Joe. "The fight was too easy, let's just go back and finish them off totally", Joe suggested and no one disagreed.

So we equipped ourselves with baseball bats, knuckle dusters and anything that made a good weapon.

We headed back to the club, by now I was feeling a bit sober. I knew what was happening, I was focused.

I was not thinking about fighting, but the girl I danced with, and finally I would be able to talk to her now, so I was happy we were going back.

When we got near to the club, I asked Joe if he could get the girl I was dancing with, if he saw her.

The boys were not there, and Joe saw the girl I was dancing with, "Yo that's the girl you were dancing with". Joe went up to your mum, a young pretty looking girl and called her over for me. The only problem was that wasn't the girl I was dancing with. When she came over I was a bit stunned, where was the big mix race girl? "Alright", she spoke in an eastern European accent, she asked me where I disappeared to and I told her I had to sort something out. We had a little chat, and that was our first meeting.

Little did I know she lived around the corner to me and she had her eye on me from day one. When she walked off, I said to Joe, "That's not the girl I was dancing with." Joe argued and said "I didn't see you dance with anyone else." Anyway I think it worked out better he did not see.

Not long after this, I was walking with Joe and Eked, going to Vikki Frost's house, along London Road, we heard some girls calling us over, Joe and Eked were not interested so I said "Boys, let me go and see." When I got to them, it was your mum and her friend Seema. We had a little chat and this time we swapped numbers. It never came to my mind that 4 years later we would be getting married. Marriage, what was that?

This was going to be my first proper relationship, in school I was scared to date, scared of being jumped by my enemies while I am with a girlfriend. Now I was in college, it was a bit different. I had a small cleaning job in Alexander House, cleaning the offices. This place was great. It was 4 hours a day and most of my friends worked there, Spoon, Leon, Matthew, Albert and at one point Spoon's brother Steve Poole. It was crazy, we caused havoc. I used to go in and sleep for the first hour. One time I was working, the phone rang and it was your mum. We spoke for a bit and I told her where I worked and so she said she would come to meet me.

At this time your mum was in year 11, she soon joined the same college I attended. I would meet her up with her friend Temi.

A few weeks into dating, your mum called me, because her Albanian friend was in trouble. She had ran away from home and mum was shouting on the phone to me, "They are going to kill her, her dad is mad." So I told them to come to my house in London Road. I had a bad feeling about this, so I called Joe just in case something was going to go down and Joe arrived at my house in no time. Shortly mum and her friend also arrived but not knowing that the Albanian brother and cousin followed them. I don't know why, but I had a large Mexican hat on and went outside to pick up the luggage and, boom, the guys appeared from nowhere, grabbed her arm and spoke in their language. It was obvious he was saying she was going with them and she was refusing, so he then pulled her by her arm and she screamed. At that point I moved closer, threw a punch, but she was in the way, my arm was blocked by her and she took most of the impact, it knocked off the jewelry she was wearing. He then reacted and started overpowering me, I pushed him back on top of a car and at that point her younger brother, who to me was too young for me to put my fist in his face, started throwing punches at me. Joe came running over pulled the older one off me and I took the little man and threw him to the floor. The older brother was showing a bit of trouble, thankfully Joe had a bottle in his back pocket, just in case and he pulled it out and it went straight on the head of the older one who then shouted in English that he is sorry and we can have her. Both of them knew it was useless fighting us. They tearfully began walking off and after all that your mum's friend went off with them. I looked at Joe we touched fists, just another fight.

My life in college was a waste of time, doing Performing Arts, I wanted to quit halfway through.

Then I did Music Tech, they kicked me out halfway through because I never attended classes, because I was always tired after working night shifts in the Westcliff casino. When I did I attend class, I was in the gardens smoking weed.

However I met good friends there, good boys compare to my school friends, Kieran Linale and Neil Brooks and they now have their own businesses. As for me life kept going downhill.

I finally hooked back up with Russell, I wanted him to meet my girlfriend but I didn't tell him. We went to the flats, your mum lived in the next road and I called her to meet up outside the flats. I told Russell to roll a joint as we chilled on the bench. Your mum was walking towards us smiling, Russell thought she was smiling at him, not knowing that, 'That's my girl', he turned to me and said "Yo check her out she's nice, oh my gosh she is smiling at me, look she is coming over." He began panicking thinking she was coming to speak to him. I remained silent, when she came over she said, "You alright babe?" and kissed me on the cheek.

Russell was like, "What? Why didn't you tell me?" His face went red and I was in tears with laughter. Now Russell had met Milena.

Our relationship was developing and so it was time to meet the family. It was New Year's Eve 2002. Shelly Biggs had a party at her dad's house; Milena did not plan to come with me as she was going to her brother and his girlfriend's party. I planned for some of my friends to come to my house before going to Shelly's dad's, so the drinking began at my house in London Road. By the time we arrived at Ditton Court, I was legless. All the boys were there; straight away I was on the dance floor, and then your mum turned up. Yes, it was a problem; I was dancing with Emmaand it got a bit too far. Mum ended up in tears and she ran to Eric, who told me off for my behaviour and I thought he was a real player. Mum wanted to leave and she was not going to leave me in that place, so we headed to her brother's party.

When we were on the road, we started arguing again about what had just happened. Some of her brother's friends saw us arguing and they went to the family and told her 3 brothers that I was beating her up. Meanwhile, some boys that I knew were walking past and we started having a chat. From nowhere Marek, the second oldest, jumped on the boy I was talking to, his name was Ice. Marek got his hand round his neck and shouted at him, "What are you doing to my sister?!" and, before I knew it, all the boys I was talking to were being pushed around and everyone was shouting, arguing and mum was crying. In my drunken mind, I was thinking; do not fight them, they're your girl's brothers, it will ruin your relationship forever. Alex, closest to your mother, was shouting at me and from nowhere the oldest one appeared, Lado, he was big and when I saw him I got worried. Then I realised he was carrying a dog, a little Yorkshire terrier, now I was not scared.

He just looked funny and he was on my side. He and his girlfriend Denisa calmed everyone down and ended the whole commotion. At least now I had met the brothers, meeting her dad was a bit easier, even though mum was worried, because she thought her dad didn't like black people, but it was just fine.

As time went by our relationship was being established. The only problem was I didn't realise how much I was becoming dependent on weed. On the other hand, Russell had a circle of new friends. I was introduced to his friends in his shared flat in York Road and together we went into the streets, looking for trouble. I didn't like his new friends; every time Russell was with his new friends, he was not the same, we didn't laugh anymore and it was as though something was missing and so we didn't see each other so much.

Every day I was asking Milena for ten pounds so that I could buy a bag of weed. Then finally I landed a job at the Westcliff casino and now I could buy my weed. I was doing night shifts and still trying to go to college and that didn't work. College was a flop, I was always sleeping or sitting on the bench, smoking weed. In the end, I was kicked out of the course and so I worked and smoked and slept.

I thought life was good, but the ganja habit got worse, I was now unable to go to work without smoking a joint. And then at work I could not concentrate, I needed a joint.

I would finish work 5am, arrive home and have a smoke, leaning out my window and I would stare at the heavens and think to myself, what's my life all about. Little did I know, my life was about to enter into a whole new chapter.

Called by God

Ephesians 1:4 *Even before he made the world, God loved us and chose us in Christ to be holy and without fault in his eyes.*

It was Saturday 5am. As I was walking out of the casino my phone rang, it was Boob aka Daniel Allen. Straight away I knew what he wanted, "Yo Chandi you finish work? Let me pick you up. I am with Charlie, Louise and Carol." Well I could not say no, why smoke alone?

Boob arrived at my house on his ped, he gave me the helmet to put on and as soon as I put the helmet on my head, the sensation of déjà vu hit me big time. Every word Boob was saying I knew he would say it.

He then started driving really fast, trying to scare me so he could joke with the others of my fear, but I couldn't fear his driving even though we almost crashed; I feared what I was experiencing, because it was not like any other time. Normally I would get the déjà vu sensation and it wouldn't last more than a minute, but this followed me all the way to Louise's house, Daniel's sister. Acting normally we laughed and smoked, but I could not help but recall every word, every move, in the end I had to go home, it was not ending, Boob ended up dropping me off. I sat on my bed thinking, "What's going on?" I took off my clothes, laid down to sleep but I could not sleep, I faced the ceiling, heard voices in my head and now went from the déjà vu sensation to premonition. As I stared into the ceiling, I saw from a bird's eye view two young lads on a motorbike, going quite fast at Hamlet Court Road junction. The bike went straight to the railway and as it crashed, the view changed to close up and one of the boy's faces went straight into my face as though he was falling directly from the ceiling. Immediately I understood there was going to be an accident and these boys were going to die on the spot. When this actually happened a few days later, I could not walk pass that accident scene and my mind was so far gone, I could not tell what was reality.

After having this vision, my mind went back to Boob and all of a sudden I got angry that he tried scaring me by mad driving, then I said these words, "He will see, for trying to f★★★ with God and me." Rapidly after saying that, I saw lightning or a symbol of electric shock in my eye and I burst into tears, I was crying like a baby. I cannot explain what took place that morning.

All I kept hearing in my mind was the word sin, sin, sin, sin. I didn't even know what the word meant.

It was now round 7am, I cried and cried then I wanted to sleep, too tired from crying. As I lay on the bed, every time I started dozing off the fear of death was so heavy on me I just started crying again. And it kept happening, it was useless trying to sleep, death was in my bed. So I called your mum, at that time she was cleaning in Marks and

Spencer's in town, being early in the morning I knew she would be up.

She picked up the phone and again I was in tears all I could say to her was that I was going to die.

She kindly came straight to my house and I cried and cried on her shoulders, she thought it was funny and cute. I realised sleep was impossible. I opened my wardrobe to put on some clothes, man, every top I touched, I saw myself wearing it, like someone was playing a video of me. All I could see was all the places I would be wearing that top at. More fear entered me, it was as though death was at arm's length.

Everything I hoped for became useless, all my dreams and desires seemed stupid. Everything I knew about life was like a dim light. And then Milena reminded me I planned to have a party that evening.

Mobile phones were not common in those days and I had invited so many people, it was not possible to cancel.

Why was this happening, the word sin kept popping in my mind, what does it mean, I knew it was a church word, so I said to Milena, we need to go to church now at 7:30am. No church building seemed to be open, the whole day I walked about like a zombie. Time was coming closer to 7:30pm, party time.

I was acting my best, trying to pull myself together, bearing in mind I did not sleep night and day.

7pm people began arriving, it was nice to see them and it felt like everything was going to be okay.

Except it was far from okay, it just got worse.

Beers were open, joints were being rolled and I decided no smoking or drinking, the thought of smoking and drinking made me sick. About ten guys sat in my room playing the playstation, a soccer game, in this game when you run really fast, your player runs with a trail of wind following him and every time I looked at that, something in my mind kept saying your spirit is full of sin. Your spirit is full of sin, that word again. I started getting paranoid, that feeling of death came over me, I was trying very hard to act normal, Shelley Biggs kept asking me, are you alright, I relised people could tell, that I wasn't myself.

The doorbell rang and it was Chris Perce with his girlfriend. Chris was the only one who took me seriously about these things. I thought to myself I can talk to him. Before he sat down or opened a beer I said, "Come into the front room, I need to talk to you." The front room was a bit quiet, I sat on the sofa, he walked in with his girlfriend, at this time the déjà vu sensation was very strong. Before he sat down he went straight to the fruit basket and now it was exactly like in my dream: he took about five seconds to decide what fruit he was going to have. He picked up an apple: I then said "I knew you were going to do that", he then looked at me with eyes wide open and said "Don't say that", I was speaking to her pointing at his girlfriend about the spiritual things. He then got scared after I said, "Bro you don't even know what's happening". He looked at me and said "Sorry I can't stay," took his girl's hand

and left. Now I was scared even more. I sat there all by myself while the party was kicking off in my room. Ad came and sat on the sofa opposite, "What's up man?" I looked at him not knowing what to say; only fear on my face, then your mum came in sat next to me and said nothing. We all sat there in silence, I then looked to the heavens and whispered, "God, what is happening to me, please tell me, what must I do, for this to stop, what do you want me to do?" Then I breathed out and the house phone rang, and we all jumped. I looked at the phone as though it was a ghost. My heart began pumping and why was that phone ringing? For some reason I was scared to pick it up, all three of us just looked at it then suddenly something said, "Pick up the phone and I will tell you what you must do."

Slowly I walked over to the phone and thought to myself, "I am just going mad, it's my friends or someone wanting mum." I picked up the phone and said, "Hello." It was quiet for a few seconds then the person started talking; what he was saying almost made me pass out, my head was spinning and after few seconds of silence, he said, "I have been given a message to tell you." I thought my heart was going to jump out of my body. How could God use the telephone? I was in fear, who was doing this? He continued talking, "I have been given a massage to tell you", "Yes please tell me." He then said "You must not eat or share cups and plates with anyone, they're unclean, you must be clean inside, because the world is going to end. A virus has come into the world, do not share your things."

As he talked more I recognized his voice, it was Uncle Willis. At the end of his message, he asked for my mum. Trying to get my breath, I told him she was not at home, he then said, "Bye." I hung up the phone, looked at Milena and Ad and said, "We cannot eat from same plates or use spoons, please tell everyone to use plastic cups." I quickly ran into the kitchen and started washing all the plates and cups and telling people, "There is a virus, please don't share anything." I looked outside and the boys made a circle and were passing a joint, I shouted out the window, "Don't pass your joint, you will get the virus, and you will die." They just laughed, thinking I was joking. Milena looked at me and she could see this was not funny or cute, "Are you alright? What did you hear on the phone?" I explained that I was told we should not eat from what other people eat from, we must find some plastic plates and cups. I don't know what your mum was thinking but the look on her face made me start crying again, at my own house party. I said to her, "Please take me away from here, I need to get out of here." "How about all these people in your house?" "I don't care," I said, "please take me away."

She rang her friend Tereza and asked if we could go and sleep at her house, so off we went just like that. I didn't even tell anyone that I was leaving and not coming back for the night. At that point nothing mattered, I was about to die or I was dead, I didn't care.

When we arrived at Tereza's she made a bed for us on the floor. I covered her pillows with tears. Every time I was dozing off, it was as though I was going to sleep and I was not going to wake up again. It was as though death was waiting for me to fall asleep. I was terrified. I tried to keep my eyes open but in the end I gave up, I remember thinking, "Death here I come", and gave up and slept.

Then I woke up. The sun was shining, I felt like a new man, I have been given a second chance.

The birds were singing, I was so happy that I was alive. Then I thought "Oh no, I wonder what my house is like." I remembered I left the house with all my friends partying. But, more importantly, I was happy to have a second chance.

Samuel, Jesus said in *Matthew 24:35* *"Heaven and earth will pass away, but my*

words   will   never   pass   away."
Do not be concerned or worry about
the things of this world. Material
things are just things, one day all these
things will pass away, they are just
things, son.

That morning that's exactly how I felt,
my eyes were opening to the wider
picture of life, my heart began asking
questions, "Why am I here? Who made
me? Where do I go when I die?" My
life turned upside down, I realized
there was more to life than meets the
eye.

For a long time I ignored my sixth
sense, but now it was right in my face.
It was time I faced the music, someone
was running this world and I needed to
know what and why.

It was here I decided I would go back to Malawi in search for the truth, to find out why this was happening to me and I wondered if my relatives in Malawi knew.

We headed back to my house, thankfully the house was fine, I just quickly tidied up, before my mum came back.

For the next few weeks, I was the strangest teen in town, I began following my instructions, 'do not share your plates or cups' and to make matters worse, I picked up the Bible to see if that had any answers for me. Without a teacher or a preacher and the guidance of the Holy Spirit, I was lost. Reading the Old Testament made matters worse than ever. Now I was told do not eat yeast, wash your clothes every night, do this, do that. I did my best to follow the law, it was killing me.

I was like a zombie – nothing was real, it was like a big dream, but I was not waking up. Premonitions were happening left and right and I started to smoke more weed than ever. Even to this day I will never understand what took place that morning, the shock in my eye that triggered everything. It was time I got to the truth.

After saving enough money, I bought my ticket for Malawi, I wanted to get to the bottom of this.

Your mum thought I was mad, bless her for putting up with me.

In June 2003 I departed for Malawi, going back home is always an exciting thing for me. Before the departure date, every night I was dreaming of the things I was going to be doing in Malawi.

One night in my dream I was in a tree watching myself, I stood there drinking a beer with my cousin. Sure enough when that day came in Malawi, I stood there with my cousin drinking beer and there was the tree, I looked up at the tree to see if I could see myself there. I began speaking with friends about all the things that were happening to me. No one knew, it just sounded silly. Malawi had no answers.

Nevertheless I was having a good time, catching up with my friends, smoking Malawi Gold, drinking chibuku and most of all being with my granddad, the greatest man on the planet.

In the end I was not getting anywhere, three months I spent there looking for the truth. But I decided that when I get back to England I would never touch alcohol again. Up to now I have kept that promise.

In October 2003 I arrived back in England and I was determined to change my ways. It was not long until I was back on slippery slope, but no alcohol, just more weed. I got my old job back in the casino.

I hadn't seen Russell for some time. His phone rang a few times and there was no answer. I had been away for three months, maybe he'd changed his number. In the end his phone stopped ringing, it was going directly to the voice mail. I had a strange feeling something bad had happened. No one seemed to know where he was, until one night I met one of his new friends, who told me what had happened. My feelings were right, Russell and his friend Justin stabbed someone and were wanted by the police.

Here it was. I had warned him, I didn't realise the extent of it, until news broke out: Russell and Justin stabbed Barry Redsull to death, over a mobile phone. My heart sank. I was confused, everything in me said I wish I had been there so I could have stopped him or done something. I knew his new friends were bad company. Yes, we did bad things but how could this have happened? I started thinking about the days when I used to tell him this would happen, so in a sense I felt guilty for knowing this was going to happen and not stopping it. This became the story of my life, I kept seeing things before they happened, but was never in control. I did try to tell my friends of these things and even told them the things they would do and none believed me. And when they did those things, they denied that I ever told them they would do them. So I gave up. Since I was never in control of it, there was nothing I could do. September 11thwas the biggest one: weeks before the planes crashed into the Twin Towers, I saw it; I saw the headlines of newspapers, I heard people talking about it and it was all in my head, clear as daylight, but what could I have done? When it happened I just felt guilty for not doing anything and all those people died.

And now there was nothing I could do, my best friend was going to jail, for something that I knew very clearly was going to happen and, yes, I told him, not just once but every time we spent time together.

This has made me realise there are things in life we cannot change that God has put things in place, which no man can change, no matter what we do.

I was very surprised at my friends' reaction over Russell's case. Only Chris and I went to visit him in jail and in court. I cannot justify the crime, but the life we lived was our lot in life. He was one funny boy, clever kid and trust me he was a good kid, his mum rang him every day, checking up on him. He would say to me "I love my mum, but she won't stop ringing me". We thought it was funny that he was a mummy's boy, ruined by the streets. Many people I know are now dead because of the street fights, or alcohol poisoning. It was our life and that's where I was heading until the call.

One crazy evening I was with Spoon (Daniel Poole) and Glen, walking along Hamlet Court Road. It was raining and I had my hoodie on, just staring at the floor. I saw so many fliers on the floor, they covered the ground, something in me was saying, pick it up, pick up the flier. I thought to myself I am not picking up a flier from the floor. As I was thinking this, Spoon picks up the flier from the floor and says "I think this is for you." He didn't know about the voice in my head that was saying pick it up, pick it up. He gave it to me and I read it. It was a flyer for the Potters House Church in Leigh-on-Sea. After I read it, I said to him "Bro, I am not going to church, especially to Leigh-on-Sea, where I have to get a bus." I screwed it up and threw it back on the floor.

A week later I was in my room bored and with nothing to do, so I decided to pray and ask God to give me answers. I said about three words and I thought I was being stupid. But something told me to go to town and I thought to myself why not. I began walking to town, when I got to near Sainsbury's in Southend, I stopped and started thinking about why I was going into town and I started laughing thinking I was crazy, I was only going to town because of the voice I was hearing. So I decided to go back home and the voice came again saying, "Look to your left", so I did and I was looking at a Christian bookshop. "Go in there", the voice carried on. By now I was laughing, all the years I had lived here, I never knew there was a Christian bookshop and the voice was saying to go in there. I really thought I was going crazy, so I decided to go home, I turned around and began walking, but I couldn't walk, it was so strange as if the wind was a brick wall and I could not walk forward and that frightened me. Therefore I crossed the road quickly and went towards the Christian bookshop. As I opened the door I was thinking to myself, "What the heck? Even the wind is getting involved."

As soon as I walked in I saw Fanuel, I have seen him around but I didn't know him. He approached me and asked me, "Are you a Christian now?" I didn't know what that meant, "Am I a Christian now?" I knew that he knew me, I'd seen him in clubs before, actually he dated Milena for a few months until I came into the picture.

He started telling me that God had changed his life and saved him from going to hell, because he now lives for Jesus Christ. Whatever he was saying, none of it made sense to me. But I liked the idea of God changing lives. Is that what I needed, the power of God, was that the answer to all the things I was experiencing? I was having a spiritual breakdown and here I was following a voice in my head.

He then asked me if I was attending any church, I said no. He then pulled out a flier for his church and to my surprise it was the same flier that Spoon picked up from the floor and gave me and said, "This is for you." My heart leapt and I took it as a sign. I started thinking to myself it's too far and I would have to get the bus. He then offered to pick me up on Wednesday evening and I agreed, in the hope that he would forget.

Sure enough Wednesday evening came and I was at Toney's house aka Artan Memolla. We were smoking weed and playing on Boob's Xbox and my phone rang, it was Fanuel. I had totally forgotten about it; he reminded me that I wanted to go to church, so I told him where I was and he came. I tried convincing Tony to come with me but he was not having it. So I jumped in, half stoned but really curious to see what it was all going to be about.

We arrived at Elmsleigh Drive, there was a small church hall. When I walked in I was quite surprised, there was only handful of people there. But one thing stood out, these folk were really genuinely happy, and I say genuinely happy because there was no alcohol, no ganja and I was used to seeing people happy because of these things, but now there was nothing and they were in church on a Wednesday night.

The pastor's wife introduced herself to me saying, "Hi my name is Pam." She had a very big smile on her. Then the pastor, he introduced himself as Nick. Why are these people happy, was the only question in my head.

The service started, Pastor Nick started singing, it didn't suit him. I stood at the back looked at the words and listened to the melody, none of it made sense. We then sat down and pastor Nic started preaching. That sermon was as though God himself was finally talking straight up. My ears were tuned in, my heart was pumping and it was as if the pastor knew my heart. God was there, everything was now being answered and now I knew what sin was. At the end of the sermon he asked people if they wanted to get right with God and repent of their sins and that God would forgive them. Those words were like water to a very thirsty soul.

I lifted up my hand to show that I wanted to pray and receive Jesus Christ as Lord and Saviour of my life. Son, Jesus Christ is Lord and Saviour of my life. He called me to the front and Fanuel came and led me through the repentance prayer. I left the altar like a new man, a totally new man and all my burdens were now lifted off me. I knew why these people were smiling: they were free from the bondage of sin.

I could not wait to tell Milena of my experience. First I went to Chris's house and as usual it was a full house and plenty of smoke. I began speaking, or let's call it preaching, "Boys you need Jesus, I feel so happy!" As I was preaching away Zack passed me a joint. Without thought, I received it and started puffing away. I mourned that the spliff was weak, it was not doing anything. He said, "It's purple haze, that's good stuff man, what are you talking about?" So I passed it on and continued preaching. I left the boys to meet Milena and I usually would never leave a room of weed to meet anyone. That alone was a sign of a new me.

I met your mum in Hamlet Court Road car park. As soon as she saw me she asked, "Why are you so happy?" I then began to tell her about this man called Jesus who died for my sins. Her reaction towards my conversion surprised me, she hated the idea of me going to church, "They're brainwashing you." For the next three months it was all about me being brainwashed and we argued every day. One day I was praying and I was making a decision that I was going to leave her and I was going to end the relationship. That week before I met her, God made it clear to me, in a very funny way, He told me not to end the relationship and if it will end, she must end it.

That was very hard for me, because she was far away from the truth, so I thought. She was going clubbing I was going to Bible studies. She used to bring temptation and I would say, no, not until we get married. We would argue, fight and argue and fight, until one day, there was a youth rally in

Walthamstow, Pastor Freddy Ruby was preaching and that sermon went straight to her heart. She came up to me and said, "I want to receive Jesus Christ." That decision changed the course of our relationship and life. We were now both saved by the grace of God and became of the same mind. "Behold, if anyone is in Christ, has become a new person. The old life is gone, a new life has begun." (2 Cor 5:17). Paul was so right when he wrote that to the Corinthians, if your life is in Christ, it is truly a new life, not an earthly life but a heavenly life.

I was set free from envy and from pursuing materialism for the sake of showing off. Eventually I was set free from the addiction of weed and from a life of violence, hate and hopelessness.

Russell would call me from jail and I shared my testimony with him, I told him God changed me and that I am not the same. He too said he started thinking about God, while he was inside and he wrote me poems and he started reading the Bible. I visited him and we both could not wait for the day of his release.

My new walk with Christ brought about new friends such as Fanuel, Daniel Turner, Mr. and Mrs. Baxter, Nana, Nathan Brown and many more. They were the pillars of the church. They helped me to grow in Christ and Pastor Nick inspired me to do something for God and my heart was set, I wanted to live for God and that was it. I didn't care if friends thought I was brainwashed, some people thought now I had gone truly mad because I wanted to live for Christ.

And so, in 2006, I proposed to Milena and 3rdSeptember 2006 was the big day.

Life was now how it was supposed to be and when Chris got saved I was over the moon. We would both talk about the things of God and study the Bible together. His room changed from a room full of clouds of smoke and from the never-ending smell of weed to a peaceful aroma and a sense of God's grace on young lives. If you came there, we did nothing but preach to you and talk about God.

What a dramatic change from fight talk, girl talk, ganja crazed, to talking only about God and His mercy.

On March 8th 2008 Russell came out of jail, but he was based in Peterborough and boy, we chatted on the phone every day, we started planning a meeting. I was to drive to Peterborough or we would meet in London and do what we did when we were younger, get a travel ticket for all zones and just go around London on top of a double Decker bus. That was the plan. Two weeks before meeting up, I received a call from his mum and nothing on the planet could have prepared me for what she was about to tell me. She said "Hi Chandi, it's Russell's mum", "Yea you alright?" thinking Russell wanted to change plans and he's got no credit to call me. "Chandi I have some bad news about Russell." I thought no way maybe he's gone back to jail. Then she paused and said "Chandi, Russell passed away, he is dead." April 13th he was pronounced dead, just weeks after coming out of jail. He died of pneumonia, I never saw that coming.

Even now that news has never sunk in. I can't stop thinking about the day we went bike riding, at Hadleigh Castle: he was riding so fast and I was trying to catch up, it was pitch black, "Russell, Russell" I shouted, "wait for me man!" He was gone. How he could see in the dark I will never know, he then came back for me, "Come man, stop riding like a girl." I remember the day he met Milena, it was so Russell to think she was going to him. We used to have such a laugh, everything was a joke with Russell, nothing was too serious and he was taken from us, still so young. At his funeral I was doing alright until I saw Adam his brother kneeling beside the coffin, then my tears rolled down like a steamed-up window and then they took away his coffin. And that was it, he was gone for good.

Samuel, it's no secret, every human being will go for good, that's why we must live for Christ, so when we die we go back to him. Only if you live for Him, if you don't live for Him, you will spend eternity in utter darkness, so live for Christ! Live for Christ. The only thing that matters in life is CHRIST.

And my life in Christ continued to grow. In November 2008, I was ordained as a pastor, at the Potter's House winter bible conference. We moved from Southend-on-Sea to Birmingham (Northfield) to pioneer a church. After almost four years of ministry, we decided to close the church, and move back to Southend.

Samuel, listen to good and wise counsel and you will do well.

Dad

And my prayer is for all those teens out there, **who know too little**. My heart is set to reaching out, to teenagers and young adults, as I truly believe if Russell and myself had more focused help and advice we would have been different people and Burry would not have been killed. I am not excusing the behaviour of violence and drugs, but for some teenagers that's all they know, and the influence of music, that promotes such behaviour, only deepens the pain of young men and women on the streets.

I love to share my testimony to young people to give them hop and a vision for the future.

If you like me to come to your School, church, or community to speak and share my testimony please do not hesitate to contact me.

Chandi Chirwa

cchirwa@tinyworld.co.uk

alettertosamuel@gmail.com

Web site

www.alettertosamuel.co.uk